XTREME INSECTS
Flies

BY S.L. HAMILTON

A&D Xtreme
An imprint of Abdo Publishing | www.abdopublishing.com

Visit us at
www.abdopublishing.com

Published by Abdo Publishing Company, a division of ABDO, PO Box 398166, Minneapolis, MN 55439. Copyright ©2015 by Abdo Consulting Group, Inc. International copyrights reserved in all countries. No part of this book may be reproduced in any form without written permission from the publisher. A&D Xtreme™ is a trademark and logo of Abdo Publishing Company.

Printed in the United States of America, North Mankato, Minnesota.
102014
012015

 PRINTED ON RECYCLED PAPER

Editor: John Hamilton
Graphic Design: John Hamilton
Cover Design: Sue Hamilton
Cover Photo: iStock
Interior Photos: AP Images, p. 29; Corbis, pp. 8-9, 28; iStock, pp. 1, 2-3, 4-5, 6-7, 12-13, 13, 14, 16, 17, 24-25, 28, 30-31, 32; Minden Pictures, pp. 10-11, 16, 24; Science Source, pp. 11, 15, 17, 18, 18-19, 20, 21, 22-23, 26-27.

Websites
To learn more about Xtreme Insects, visit: booklinks.abdopublishing.com
These links are routinely monitored and updated to provide the most current information available.

Library of Congress Control Number: 2014944883

Cataloging-in-Publication Data

Hamilton, S.L.
 Flies / S.L. Hamilton.
  p. cm. -- (Xtreme insects)
ISBN 978-1-62403-689-7 (lib. bdg.)
Includes index.
1. Housefly--Juvenile literature.   I. Title.
595.77--dc23

                                    2014944883

Contents

Flies

Flies are a nuisance insect. They surround us when we're eating outdoors. Some bite. Some carry diseases. However, flies are an important part of our ecosystem. Some feed on and clean up dead animals. Others pollinate flowers. Many become food for birds, bats, amphibians, fish, and other large insects. Flies help maintain a balance in our world.

XTREME FACT – *There are more than 100,000 species of true flies. True flies are part of the order Diptera, meaning "two wings." These flies have one set of wings and one set of "halteres," or balancing organs.*

Body Parts

Flies, like all insects, are made up of three parts: head, thorax, and abdomen. They have one pair of developed wings. Their second set of wings have formed into knob-like parts called halteres, which help keep the fly balanced.

Head

Large eyes allow flies to see all around them.

Antennae

Flies have sponge-like mouthparts that are used to suck up liquids. Some flies bite, but only to obtain liquid food, such as blood. None are equipped to bite and chew food.

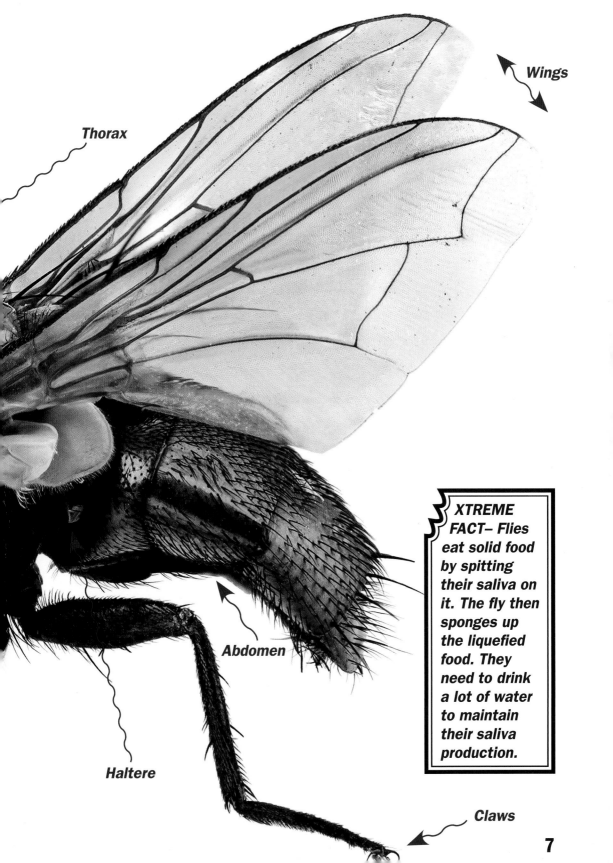

Wings

Thorax

XTREME
FACT– Flies
eat solid food
by spitting
their saliva on
it. The fly then
sponges up
the liquefied
food. They
need to drink
a lot of water
to maintain
their saliva
production.

Abdomen

Haltere

Claws

Housefly

Houseflies are part of nature's cleanup crew. They eat all types of spoiled food and decaying matter. Their eggs are laid on feces. When the eggs hatch, the worm-like larvae eat the poop. It's disgusting, but important work. Because houseflies land and eat in dumps, sewers, and garbage piles, bacteria and disease are picked up and transported by their legs, body hairs, and mouths wherever they go. This is why they are sometimes referred to as "filth flies." While their job is important, it's best that houseflies remain outdoors.

XTREME FACT– Houseflies may carry more than 65 different diseases, including salmonella, typhoid fever, dysentery, cholera, and tuberculosis.

Blowfly

Blowflies have a beautiful metallic appearance, but they are attracted to dead things. They clean up dead carcasses. In fact, police investigators sometimes use the various stages of blowfly development to help them determine how long a corpse has been dead.

Blowflies find and lay eggs within seconds of a creature's death. The smell of decomposing flesh attracts female blowflies from a distance of up to .62 mile (1 km). Within a day, the fly eggs hatch and the larvae emerge. The worm-like maggots burrow into the dead meat. In about a week, they crawl from their dead host to find a dark, dry place to finish growing. In another two weeks, the fly emerges from its pupa stage and flies off.

Blowfly maggots feeding on a carcass.

XTREME FACT– *Four thousand blowflies can live off the carcass of a single dead rat.*

Crane Fly

Is that the biggest mosquito you've ever seen? No, it's a crane fly. The long-legged insects do not have a proboscis, nor do they bite. Females lay eggs through a long ovipositor, but it only looks like a stinger. The larvae of some species of crane flies are pests. They live in the soil and eat the roots of crops, harming or killing the plants.

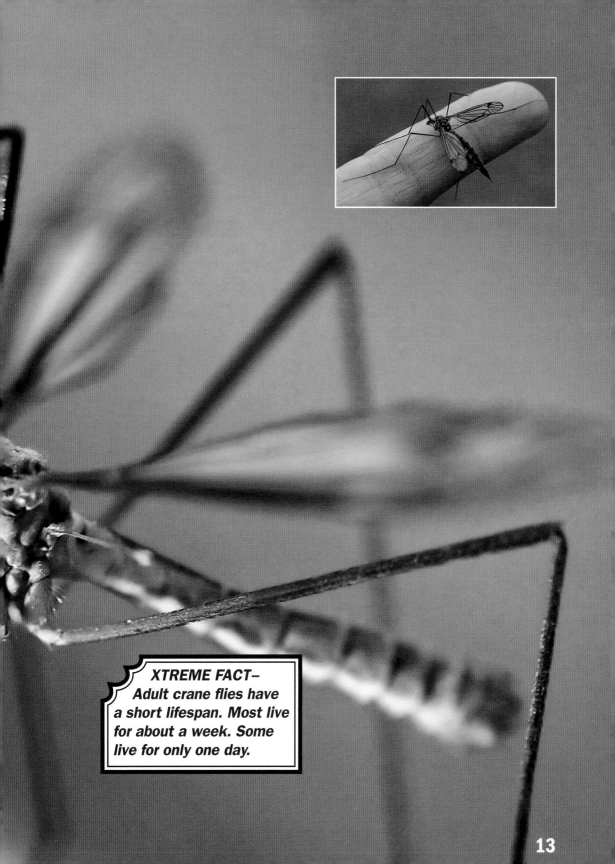

XTREME FACT–
Adult crane flies have a short lifespan. Most live for about a week. Some live for only one day.

Flower Fly

Flower flies use their wasp-like appearance to frighten would-be predators. However, these flies have no stinger and no venom. Like bees, they do an excellent job of pollinating flowers as they move from plant to plant eating harmful aphids. They are welcomed by gardeners.

XTREME FACT– Flower flies are often called hoverflies because they can hover in the air like a helicopter.

Horsefly

Female horseflies have a painful bite. Their knife-like mandibles cut into flesh. Cattle, horses, and humans provide tasty blood that a female laps up with a sponge-like mouthpart. In addition, the saliva of these flies can cause an allergic reaction. This results in itchy welts and swelling, much like a mosquito bite.

Deerfly

Deerflies are similar to horseflies. They are slightly smaller, but just as much of a pest. They begin searching for meals after mating. Females bite into flesh to draw blood. They need the blood to develop their eggs. Female deerflies lay between 100 to 800 eggs on a leaf or plant, creating another large generation of biting flies.

XTREME FACT– Male deerflies only eat pollen and nectar. They are distinguished from females by their large eyes, which touch each other. Males help pollinate plants.

Tsetse Fly

Tsetse flies are native to Africa. They can be tiny killers. A tsetse fly is armed with a long proboscis. It stabs humans and animals in order to drink their blood. If the blood contains the parasite that causes African sleeping sickness, or trypanosomiasis, the tsetse fly may infect the next creature it bites with the disease.

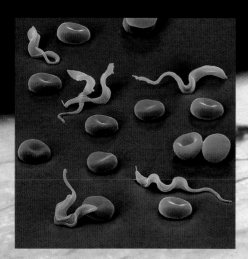

Left: Ribbon-like parasites called Trypanosoma brucei attacking human red blood cells. Tsetse flies carry the parasite in their saliva and infect people by biting them.

If left untreated, a person can die from African sleeping sickness. Modern medicine has brought about a sharp decline in the number of infected people. However, each year thousands of people become sick with the disease.

XTREME FACT– At rest, a tsetse fly folds its wings one on top of the other on its abdomen.

Mosquitoes are the deadliest creature in the world. Female mosquitoes use a long proboscis to bite and suck blood to get the protein they need to create eggs. If they bite sick people, they can carry such diseases as malaria, dengue fever, yellow fever, and encephalitis. Mosquitoes kill more than 725,000 people each year by transmitting disease from person to person. Although deadly, mosquitoes are an important part of our world, providing food for bats, birds, amphibians, and wasps.

To find their prey, female mosquitoes look for clouds of carbon dioxide—a gas that all humans breathe out. They can detect carbon dioxide up to 75 feet (23 m) away, and keep circling until they find their next meal.

XTREME FACT– A female mosquito's wings beat 300 to 600 times per second. This creates the whine people hear.

Robber Fly

The robber fly is also called the assassin fly. It waits for prey to pass by, then grabs its unsuspecting dinner in midair. Once caught, grasshoppers, dragonflies, beetles, bees, and other insects are injected with the robber fly's paralyzing saliva. The saliva also contains enzymes that digest the prey's insides. The robber fly then enjoys sucking up the liquefied insides through its proboscis.

A robber fly feeding on a captured bee.

Tachinid Fly

Tachinid flies lay eggs on or near live caterpillars. The flies hatch as worm-like maggots and eat their way into the caterpillar, leaving the most vital organs for last. Although gruesome, tachinid flies are a gardener's friend. They eat pests that harm plants grown for humans.

Left: Tachinid fly pupae next to an empty moth pupa.

Flies in Medicine

Although flies often spread disease, they may also help people. Maggot therapy uses hungry, disease-free fly larvae to help clear away dead and infected tissue. Maggots are not attracted to healthy flesh. When one diseased area is all eaten, they look for another area. Blowflies are usually used in maggot therapy. Their saliva dissolves the dead tissue. It also disinfects the area by killing bacteria. Maggots happily lap up the dead tissue. Patients with burns, non-healing sores, and gangrene (dead) tissue can expect to be well on their way to healing in just two to four days.

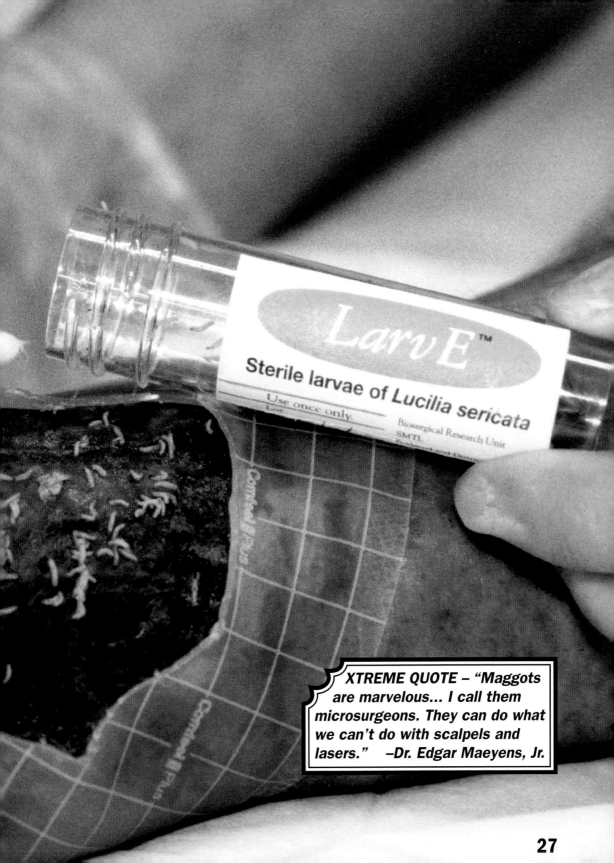

XTREME QUOTE – "Maggots are marvelous... I call them microsurgeons. They can do what we can't do with scalpels and lasers." –Dr. Edgar Maeyens, Jr.

Can You Eat Them?

Fly pupae

Flies not only carry bacteria and disease, but they often land on plants that have been sprayed with chemicals. Eating maggots or adult flies can make a person sick. However, fly pupae, the stage when maggots rest and eventually emerge as adult flies, are edible. Pupae have a hard shell. They look like tiny red pills and are full of protein and high levels of iron.

Black soldier fly larvae risotto

Glossary

ANTENNAE
Long, thin appendages on an insect's head that act as sensors for such things as vibrations or scents. Flies use their antennae to navigate and detect danger.

BACTERIA
Single-celled organisms that often cause illness and disease in humans.

FECES
An animal's waste matter, poop.

LARVA
A newly hatched insect, usually wormlike in shape, that has yet to change into its adult form.

MANDIBLES
Strong, beak-like mouth organs that are used for grabbing and biting food.

PROBOSCIS
In insects such as mosquitoes, a long, sucking mouthpart that is tube-shaped and flexible. Mosquitoes use it to puncture the skin of prey in order to feed on blood.

Pupa

An insect's immature phase between the larva and adult stage. While the insect changes to an adult (goes through metamorphosis), it may be totally encased in a shell-like covering, such as a chrysalis or cocoon.

Species

A group of living things that have similar looks and behaviors, but are not identical. They are often called by a similar name. For example, there are more than 100,000 species of flies.

Thorax

The middle section of an insect's body between the head and the abdomen.

Index